KATIJ

FROM SPHERE TO SKY

THE SHAREDPEN OFFICIAL

Made with ♥ on the Notion Press Platform
www.notionpress.com

The SharedPen Official is an organisation, that solely works for the betterment of the society in terms of Art. It provides the platform to all sorts of budding writers, where they get a chance to shape their craft better. The SharedPen Official comes with the motive to bind the artists together, irrespective of gender, age, caste and creed. The Organisation comes up with different prompts and contests inorder to engage the generation of all sorts, hooked up with creativity. To obliterate "Empty mind is devil's workshop" it organises talkshows with renowned personalities who talks about most common prevailing issues in any society. The Organisation conducts other live shows, where usually the unique talent is celebrated. The SharedPen applauds that special spark within the people around and makes them fundamentally unique from the rest of the world. Art for Art sake!

Art knows no prejudice, art knows no boundaries, art doesn't really have judgement in it's purest form. So just go, just go.

Contents

Publishing-in-support

Publishing-in-support-of,

The Sharedpen Publication.
The voice of unpublished writings.
Instagram handle: @thesharedpenofficial | thesharedpenofficial@gmail.com@gmail.com

---

Preface

"Katij" is dedicated to each soul, who knows how to stay in shell and become a pearl. It symbolises the woman, who has burnt down into ashes due to the Patriarchy and her crippled mindset. The bruised woman has faced many ill treatments, but eventually she raised herself with such strength and confidence that she initiated to be the sparkling diamond. The women of every age bears the patience, which no man of any age could possess! The Lord has blessed her with immense strength that she knows how to treat her scars and emerge as a 'she-roes' . This book contains fifteen poetic and prose pieces, written by different authors on the different shades of the life of women including her status and strength. The book is a must read for every reader, of any age or religion! The book takes you to the journey of a woman from the parts of sphere to the horizons and the skies. The woman is as fragile as a glass but as strong as an iron! She carries the charisma, which great poets and novelists have expressed in their mornings and nights, in their writings and in speeches. Yes! (he)roes in (she)roes

Acknowledgements

With profound exhilaration, the SHARED PEN Official expresses its gratitude to all the writers who took part in the writing competition conducted for bringing out yet another anthology solemnly dedicated to the "sinf e aahan-The WOMEN". Our heartiest felicitations to those who made their place in the anthology. Our relentless efforts to bring to front the unexplored talent will continue with the support and cooperation of our fan following. It is an immense pleasure to acknowledge the writers who made an emotional, creative and intellectual effort and placed their names in the anthology.

Women writing for women is acceptable but when a men writes for a women, it is exceptional! So we owe a great deal of humbleness to our male writers for this anthology. Seeing our brethren toiling hard with full compassion and zest is an euphoric feeling for us and we pledge to continue serving our society with the best possible attempts from our team to reach to every unsung hero.

CHAPTER ONE

Entry no.1

About the Author:

Muntaher Manzoor is 19 years old writer from Sopore, area of Baramulla, Jammu And kashmir . He has completed his intermediate education in Medical stream from Govt. Boys Higher Secondary school, Sopore. Currently he is pursuing B.A. Poltical science from Aligarh Muslim University. His desire is to be a civil servant and serve the society for all noble initiatives. He has been writing novels and poems from his childhood and is much inspired by William Shakespeare and J.K. Rowling. He is the co -author of many anthologies and presently he is writing a book namely " 7 DAYS OF HEAVEN ". He is a columnist providing articles to different newpapers of the valley. He is the part of "DIYA DELHI FLAGSHIP" which aims to provide free education to poor and orphans throughout the country. As a writer, he believes writing is a sword for a writer to layout different commodities affairing in the world. His family plays a vital role in fullfilling his dreams. He is the beauty with the brains as he is involved in certain other good activities as well. He always write articles on the depressed sections of the society. His hobbies includes reading books, playing

cricket, watching good stuff and to host events.

Decades back, when this civilised sphere used to be gender beast,
This high society was prevaded with vexation towards the portent of goodness.
Despite animating in this colourfull globalization, women ache through the imbalance of lifesytle.
In the secular module; child marriage, sati pratha, dumb to widow remarriage ,
Devdasi system were wounded tears of fed river.
Era of swap came ! when the women potrayed their gloss orb in this inequity globe ,
The lassie protagonist achieved the heights of success.
They were now pioneer in their own upright.
Hush! the inequalities are still going on with the lads, throughout the globe.
The poet desire to spot ambitious lads on same ladder of gender.

CHAPTER TWO

Entry no.2

About the Author:

Ali Ashhar is a poet, short story writer, philosopher and columnist. At the age of 22, he received India Prime 100 Authors Award and was chosen as Best Debut Author by The Indian Awaz in the year 2021. His poems, short stories and articles have been published in the UK, the USA, Ireland, Turkey and several other countries around the world.

However, his journey on the road to become an author wasn't smooth. He hails from the city of Jaunpur in Uttar Pradesh and is one of the few English authors of his town. After completing his high school studies, he continued with science to study further. He was sent to Kanpur, a city which is the coaching hub for exams like JEE and NEET in Uttar Pradesh. Finding himself in a crowd of 500-600 students attending IIT coaching along with him was a new experience for him altogether. With the passage of time, he found difficulty in continuing with science as he was struggling with his studies. He wrote his JEE-Mains and State's engineering entrance exam in the year 2016 which resulted into a disaster. With this setback, he decided to introspect within and asked himself what went wrong. He found out that instead of science his passion always lied in literature. He decided to mend his decision and became an undergraduate literature student. His decision was mocked by several people including his own relatives that how someone from preparing for IIT went on to study arts. This situation definitely impacted him as a person, but he decided not to back down. He started writing poems, a love he developed while studying literature. During lockdown in April 2020, he started sharing his poems on social media platforms and many literary pages from England, US, and around the world featured him on their page. Later that year, his first poem was published in an anthology by one of the most followed publishing houses in India namely, Writer's Pocket. He went on to co-author several other anthologies, before his first collection of poems was published in June 2021. He won four literary awards for his debut book.

He continued to explore the realms of writing and wrote several articles and short stories which was acclaimed nationally and internationally. He believes that life is not what happens to us, but it's how we deal with what happens with us.

Writing a poem I reminisce,
I owe it to a woman
who taught me, how to write.
Heaven lies underneath her feet,
for she is a divine reflection of God's love— emphasizes,
our beloved Prophet.
A Learned man knows wonder nevertheless a learned woman does miracle mellifluously—

blessing her progeny prodigiously
with the nectar of knowledge.
In the galaxy of faith,
love knows not to fade away
for true lovers reunite in Jannah.
A wife is known as other half of husband
who completes his existence
in this world
and have a rendezvous with him.
In the hereafter,
the best of a man
is the best to his other half-
in the words of our beloved Prophet.
Our beloved Prophet didacticize—
blessed is the lady,
whose first child is a daughter
and blessed is the man
who protects her and raises her well
don't you know what Fatima was to him.

CHAPTER THREE

Entry no.3

About the Author:

Dr. Farkhanda Rahman is a Veterinary doctor by profession. She has always been fond of writing. She is a columnist for various J&K based newspapers and magazines. She has contributed her articles in various anthologies. She is a part of the Book " Breaking The Stereotypes, Inspiring Women of Kashmir." She has won a certificate of merit in the National Article Writing Competition from Lucknow, India. In addition, she is a growing calligraphy artist and has won several certificates from the online Indian Art Contests. She is the only female veterinarian to visit a highland for treatment of an animal. She has been awarded several times by J&K Youth Development Forum as an inspiring woman. In addition she is a bibliophile, nature and wildlife lover. The author could be reached on Instagram @artyouheart

The hand that rocks the cradle is the hand that rules the world" says William Ross. Every single being in this cosmos is from a woman, fostered by a woman, ally's a woman, nurtures a woman (daughter) and can unearth heaven beneath the feet of a woman. A matron is man's helpmate and home-maker, swift to life and flambé to boredom, tranquil to distress and covertly a money saver. No one other than a woman knows the art of mothering. She is the first school of all noble laureates. During his mouldable period, a mother uncovers and nurtures child's special traits, aptitude and attitude, coaches him the laws of race, manners of men, moral code and the social heritage. She is a curator and organises the home. In the looming intricate social rundown, women aren't mere harbingers of peace but the begetter of power and the symbol of progress. The hustles of life demand collaboration not competition between men and women.

"Extremists have shown what frightens them most: A girl with a book" says Mala Yousufzai. The overall literacy rate in Jammu and Kashmir it is 77.3% (85.7% male and 68% female). Patriarchy (male domination in both private and public spheres) features a strong and intelligent woman as a disruption to social order than an integral part of it. Some are treated as fragile beauty of home supposed to stay indoors while others are involved in early marriage, child labor and trafficking. Moreover, educating a daughter is expressed as to take expenses for someone else's benefit as they have to leave one day ("akher chi kuur lukhund maal"). More than three quarters of the female population remain out of the work force while those who are a part of it earn less than male worker (19% less in India) mainly due to parameters such as lesser willingness to clock in late evening hours or the likelihood of seeking maternity leave. The gender wage gap leads to quitting of jobs and hence women unemployment. One out of three women in the world encounters physical or sexual assault in her lifetime, making domestic violence boundless yet least reported human rights abuse that has gripped the whole world. Islam with its glory saved and sublimed women 1400 years ago. The first woman in Islam Hazrat Khadeja (RA) is the respected example of women empowerment. The verses of Holy Quran affirm the invaluable status of women at different stages of her life (daughter, wife and mother). From whom we need validation when the Creator of this universe has dedicated one whole Chapter (An-Nisa:4) of Holy Quran to women. The word 'Women Empowerment' itself implies women are not powerful enough-they need to be empowered. Empowering women is to empower a nation. Provision of fundamental rights is the foundation stone of empowerment. The lockdown of COVID-19 caged the sapiens but was an eye-opener for those who seek. In Jammu and Kashmir, there has been sprouting of independent buds since the lockdown. Artists, writers, content creators, online and offline business ventures are upbeat and the shining feather of the cap is female folk taking the major share. Social media handles have been the main supporting platforms for presentation, connection and boom of the women tribe. In the logbook of gender discrimination, victim is actually the culprit. Oftentimes a mother wants her first child to be a son. Women in house and society always try to bring down another woman (having only daughters). Till the walls of disparity are high within us, gender bias will be glamoured. The sun of equality and empowerment will rise when we follow a healthy womanhood, motherhood, and sisterhood, the duties of which may embark:

1. Validate her self-expression: when she breaks the cocoons of silence about her personal or professional states, listen and support for her mental and emotional

wellbeing.

2. Check your assumptions: The unconscious bias of one woman against other based on race, age, physical abilities, body type, and socioeconomic background needs to be recognised and overcome to uplift the women in same field.

3. Prioritize her solitude: Solitude is bliss for times because it helps to unplug from the routine and gives the opportunity to reinvigorate our mind, body and surroundings.

4. Pass the mic: Sometimes empowering yourself means stepping back and allowing someone else into the spotlight," Jawed-Wassel. If you have an opportunity but the other woman is more aware about the issue, pass the mic!

5. Invest in women-run businesses and share and teach your skills

6. Being SEEN is empowering. Women do a lot of organisational and emotional labour which frequently goes unpaid and unnoticed. We can thank our mothers for the tasty meals they prepare, can't we?

7. Dimming someone else's light does not make yours shine brighter. Sponsor other women. I don't want to protect women rights and raise the slogan of women empowerment but I want to create a world where women rights need no protection.

CHAPTER FOUR

Entry no.4

About the Author:

Mansha Harco was born and brought up in Srinagar, Kashmir. Since childhood she was interested in reading books and writing poems. She has interned with several NGOs and believes that if we have the privilege to help someone, we must. A space enthusiast with a passion for research and technology, she is currently pursuing B. Tech. She has been a member of NBT India Readers Club since 2015 and has a proficient experience at blogging and content writing. After her seven word story was among top 3 in a contest, she was given a chance to work for her first anthology. With her Profound interest in literature, she has been co-authoring anthologies under different publications since then. She is fond of learning languages and studying their literature as well. She has been writing poems and writeups in English, Urdu and Kashmiri as well. Apart from her interest in literature and science, she is fond of teaching students. She believes good education can change anyone and the dying interests in reading and writing are due to lack of exposure at schools. She loves experimenting different genres for her writeups and poems as well. She

has a variety of interests that she uses to maximize her potential and stay abreast in achieving goals. She could be reached on Instagram handle @mansha_harco

Empowerment' as Collins define, is an authority or power given to someone to do something. In an era, where empowering a particular sect or gender is misjudged as core centric epitome of excuses or reasons put forth by a sect for their own benefits, it still remains a focus to reach out to people and preach the true meaning of empowerment. Empowerment means people having power or control over their own lives, whether it be a gender, a sect or a cult. Empowerment means uplifting people, the basic term of empowerment is never gender centric. As a person, if feelings of being underprivileged strikes you, then there is the need to empower. Empowering doesn't mean that you are less and somewhat require someone's help. It refers to just lending a hand to someone who has not been given the right and equal status by the society and requires to claim the same. When we talk about women empowerment, we don't refer to empower her with some super natural or different or special abilities rather what we refer to is providing her the status of being equal.

Empowering women doesn't mean that women require to be provided a special power because they are less or something. On the other hand, we live in a society where we are made to feel like women are less, they hold a low status in the society, so we need to give them the hand in order to let them rise to the level of equality again. That's true women empowerment. Empowering them in the spheres of life where they are made to feel like being less in power and potential. Empowering women means to make her know herself, her true worth. She is already empowered but society makes her feel otherwise, so we just have to let her realize that she is equal to the other gender. That's true essence of empowerment. Women have been subjected to many crimes. Female infanticide and foeticide have been prevalent since ages. In every sphere of life, women has faced discrimination. At homes, at public places, at work and where not! If Mars becomes colonized, I hope there is no such thing like discrimination. Even in fields of study and research women have been discriminated on being less competitive and knowledgeable. All this arises from the mentality and thinking of people which needs to be altered.

Women have been robbed of their basic fundamental rights and all these things have been camouflaged under the name of culture, religion, traditions and what not. Women are made to believe that they are less and require help of these terms such as empowerment and feminism, but in reality they need to be realized that are equal. Women are no less potentiated than men. They hold no less status in the society. If we treat people differently, the difference will never ever be. We need to treat people with a sense of equality and equity.

CHAPTER FIVE

Entry no.5

About the author:

Shah Bisma Manzoor is from Bijbehara Anantnag. She has completed masters in English Literature and Political Science. Currently, she is working as a Vice Principal of a higher secondary institute in Bijbehara.

Writing has been her passion right from childhood. She would scribble snippets and gradually gained a little mastry on holding words. Though to attain perfection, she feels she has still to travel a lot. She Was in Grade Seventh, when she wrote her first poem. The poem was about parents which got published in DAILY GREATER KASHMIR. That accomplishment encouraged her to write more and more.

She has compiled hundreds of poems, contributed in twenty anthologies and authored " THE KING OF MY KINGDOM." Currently, she is working on another book that will be published soon. She is a frequent contributor of an online Journal "The PERIODICAL". The author could be reached on Instagram handle @tranquil_colette

From the ashes,I will rise again.
Like a phoenix, up from its debris.
The four walls will no longer deter me from
the heights of success, I will achieve.
The chauvinists surely, i will fall prey to
My strength within me, will come to my rescue!
An incarnation of determined spirit I will be,
No longer will I fumble by the manly figure.
My spirit is high, so is my resolution,
my resolve will suppress the fears within me.
My tears too have reconciled with me,
a strong ocean of ambitions will arise.
You tried to put me to deep slumber.
Alas! my ingenuity woke me up from the ignorance. My
incentive mind and the ambitious soul,
summoned me to the court of planned plans.
My heart comprehended the skills in me
with a vehement smile, it boosted me to move ahead.
I have stood up, to speak up, for me.
No longer, i will look back to be a victim of taunts.
Hey!
throw at me, all sorts of curses and abuses,
I Pray!
Let my paths I tread on,
Create an elysian field for you all.
Hark Thee!
From the ashes, i will rise again.

CHAPTER SIX

Entry no.6

About the Author:

Shah Mursaleen Manzoor, hailing from Bijbehara Anantnag, has pursued masters in English and Political science. Right from her childhood, she would jot down words in broken English and that used to delight her. She finds writing a panacea, for her aches and mood swings. She has successfully published " THE KING OF MY KINGDOM" a book about the sacrifices made by a father. She believes that her instincts into writing boost her intellect and she tends to dive deep into the fantasies. She accepts her father as an inspiration and dedicates her every success to him. She finds nature a motivating factor for her whenever she feels gloomy or low. Her vision towards life is that of a philanthropic one - finding eternal happiness in helping others be it by just passing a smile to make someone's day or handing a candy to a poor kid who can't afford it. For her, service to mankind is a means of earning an irreplaceable reward here in this world and in Hereafter.

She believes that adding spark to someone's dark moments is the best way to brighten one's own life. She adds, " Being mortals, one has to be prepared for the

accountability in the Hereafter and being sincere, helpful and honest is what can secure one's Aakhira. Since we are surrounded with betrayal, hypocrisy all around, it is our duty to be mindful of treacherous elements and protect our community from the same."

Her main aim is to spread happiness in whatever way she can. She finds it an obligatory duty to help the abandoned ones and the destitute. Observing nature and writing is her hobby. She feels, nature teaches us discipline. The kaleidoscopic view of the Nature fascinates her.

She ends by extending a message that everyone should utilise their talent, whatsoever it is, for the betterment of mankind. She hopes that writers tend to write such things that can motivate the demotivated ones and give a direction to the deviated paths.

I will recreate the lost identity,
Amid the chaotic chaos.
In the phantomic male dominance,
I will recreate my lost identity.
My vanquished strength,
the terrified dreams,
acting like an armour in the battle field.
My determined originality will be my battle pride.
Hey listen!
I will recreate my lost identity.
The diminished spirits in me,
the sunken eyes and the lost smile!
Will sue you to the court of my shattered dreams. Where
my suppressed voice will speak,
my silenced aspirations will yell
and the gloomy laughter will dance.

Listen!
I will recreate my lost identity.
Visualising my success dancing,
seeing me creating a gem out of the tromented one. Your arrows of dominance and the fangs of jelaousy will hit me hard.
But my perseverance will not give up.
I will recreate my lost identity.
An empowered one, i will take rebirth!

CHAPTER SEVEN

Entry no.7

About the Author:

Sidii Safiya Rafiq hailing from Khrew- an area of district Pulwama, Jammu and Kashmir India, is born to Mr Mohammad Rafiq and Sadiya Banu. She is the sibling of a single brother. She has completed her elementary and Secondary education from Light House Public School and Government Girls Higher Secondary schooS Khrew respectively. She has completed her graduation from Government Degree College for Women, M.A road Srinagar and did her Masters in Economics from Indira Gandhi National open University. She has qualified UGC NET and few CBT and written exams conducted by JKSSB, JKPSC. Currently she is preparing for competitive exams and besides teaches of secondary classes. She has been a part of various debates, painting and poetry competitions. She has always been supported and appreciated by teachers, authors, poets and her family. She is fond of making paintings and started writing in twelfth class. She received certificates and awards from schools and colleges for her paintings. She has a collection of written and recorded articles, summaries, poetry and prose pieces, and

unpublished yet. She writes in English, Urdu, Kashmiri and Punjabi. She writes on different themes including Phantasy, Civil andpm Political issues. The Co-author could be reached on Instagram handle @sidiisafiya852

She is a woman,
The body that carries another sawol.
The Womb which sustains generations.
She is a woman taking care of relations,
suffers nine months, but never chokes.
The one who gives you recognition,
the chance to live with ambition,
takes away from you all the pain,
struggles all but never complain.
She manages your home,
doing this all alone, forgets rest.
She has the capability but she digest.
Shoulders responsibility takes the test.
You marry her, take dowry from her,
But why don't you worry about her?
You tell her the stories of Prince and Princesses,
but still under the walls?
Why don't you let them be free?
The pain they suffer you agree,
bravely takes home burden,
Why then the relief for them,
is
so pricy?

CHAPTER EIGHT

Entry no.8

About the Author:

Madiha Salati is a passionate writer, student and an aspiring author. She has been writing since childhood and has now developed her skills to become an experienced writer. She enjoys writing about different themes related to literature, psychology and lifestyle. Madiha loves to tell stories through her writing that reflect the emotions of human life in a deep and meaningful way. As an aspiring author, she looks forward to publishing her first novel in the near future.

Madiha had to face a difficult period in her life. She met an accident that left her bedridden for almost 6 months. Despite this, Madiha did not give up and eventually recovered. Her story serves as an inspiration to many, showing that no matter how hard the situation may seem, it is possible to overcome it with courage and determination.

She was determined to not let her injuries stop her from anything so she started writing an auto-biography "Bed Rest ".

Madiha is also into a start-up business that specializes in customized gifts. She offers clients the opportunity to

create personalized and unique gifts for their loved ones. Whether it's a birthday, anniversary any accomplishment or special occasion, customers can choose from an array of customizable gifts that will make any special moment even more memorable. With Madiha Salati's wide array of products and dedicated customer service, customers can be sure that their gift is exactly what they had in mind. Summarizing Madiha's personality is Writing for the soul. Seeking to inspire, transform and create through words. Aspiring to make a mark in the world of literature and business. The co-author could be reached on Instagram handle @madiha_writes_

Find the brave girl in you,
Learn to lead your destiny.
Make a beautiful fantasy!
I have died in a pain of it,
still i have learnt to dance in it.
May be, no one can provide me the helping hand,
I will still emerge to come out as a rainbow band.
You will fail and you will fall,
You have to get up and break the wall.
Journey won't be smooth,
But you have to be strong and sooth.
Learn to stand for epiphany,
People will make it euphony.
Let them provoke you,
Get up and evoke the hue.
They will put you down
Get up and show them your crown!

CHAPTER NINE

Entry no.9

About the Author:

Nusrat shapoo is from the town of springs that is Anantnag. As far as their educational qualification is concerned, she have done masters in English Literature through the "seat of learning" which is Kashmir university. After that, she did B.ed degree at Rehmati college of Education Anantnag. Later, she got selected in the M.ed program through distance mode from Kashmir university as well. Plus, she possesses a diploma in Information Technology (IT). She adds " my educational success; not only educational success but everything; owes to my parents. It is only because of Allah's will and hard work of my parents that they provided me the opportunity to achieve my triumph. Otherwise, it was impossible because everyone in society doesn't support girl education thinking that it is a waste of money "

After completing her education, she worked as a college contractual and a teaching assistant at GDC Doru Anantnag for two years. She have worked as a contractual English lecturer in a higher secondary as well. Moreover, she have worked as a contractual teacher for two years in a school.

As far as her pursuits are concerned, she likes to read books and likes to write about small happenings in life. She likes gardening and is a great admirer of nature. She likes woods and spending time there in the lap of nature. She like tranquility and serenity. She wants to learn more and more and thinks learning is an endless process it should never be given up.

She believe in Allah(s.w.t) and agrees Allah is the best planner and plans the best for His creatures. She could be reached at Shapoonusrat@gmail.com and her Instagram handle is @nusratshapoo

Women empowerment means giving equal rights and authority to women. women should be financially independent and they should be given equal opportunities for education employment and decision-making. The woman is an independent personality in Islam. Islam has given the highest place to women. It is well explained in our religious book "Quran" that Paradise lies under the mother's feet. From this, we can understand the place of women in Islam. But females are said to be burdens on families. They are deprived of education. As Prophet Muhammad (S.A.W)has conveyed : "The pursuit of knowledge is a duty of every Muslim man and Woman". Some elements in society assume females as inferior to men. Females suffer from the very childhood, they cannot step out of their houses freely because street dogs are on the prowl!!!...to follow them, harass them, and they spend their whole lives in fear. Females are always harassed and tortured. Because of this harassment, some girls have left their education and jobs, and they have confined themselves indoors. Their misers and sufferings do not end here..after marriage in-laws treat them as slaves. They are deprived of food, clothing and basic facilities of life. They treat their daughter-in-law as a slave (nosh mahnew in Kashmiri language). A girl is not allowed to continue her education after marriage and if she does so, in-laws mock her day and night as if he had sinned; making her life miserable. As a result of this ill behavior, she becomes a victim of depression affecting her health. It is pointed out in our religious book "the best among you is he, who has the best manner, and the one who is well mannered and nice to his wife". To empower a woman she should be given equal opportunities. She should be encouraged to study as much as she wants to. She should be given the chance to make decisions about herself. She should be given opportunities to work independently to become financially stable. She should be encouraged to study after marriage. She should be given equal opportunities and should be encouraged to carry out an enterprise. She should not be considered weak and powerless. If a woman is empowered society will prosper in all facets.

CHAPTER TEN

Entry no.10

About the Author:

Bintul Islam is an author, a poet and researcher, who hails from the small hamlet 'Thokerpora' in district Budgam. She has graduated in B.A English (Honors) and done her masters in (English literature and language) from University of kashmir. She has persued Bachelor's of Education (B.Ed) from University of Kashmir as well. She has completed Masters of Philosophy (M.Phil) in English Literature from Annamalai University, Tamil Nadu. She has submitted her thesis under the title " Lyricism and Feminism : A Comparative study of Habba Khatoon and Sarojini Naidu. " She is the author of Pain and Panacea and has been a part of two anthologies. Inspired by British poet George Gordon Byron and Kashmiri poets like lal Ded and Habba Khatoon, her aim is to play with words and disseminate the Lyrics to every heart.

Bintul Islam has started to write back in 2011. Writing came to her just an epiphany. She used to write on nature, love, pain, separation and social issues. She believes " Be a warrior, not a worrier ". She believes Life is a bed of roses, the only condition that stands is, accept thorns as

you accept petals. She dedicates her poetry to the loved ones and her research to the land of Kashmir. She has won many online national and international contests. She could be reached at bintul134@gmail.com and on Instagram @bintul_islaam.

Takhleeq-e-Khuda, O Woman!

Takhleeq e Khuda, O woman!
Today, I write the happiest lines.
In the moonlit night, among stars,
I saw you dancing in the strings of Rabab.
Playing with the melody, bringing harmony,
to the holes of flute and hearts of many.
Kul e kayanaat for the bosom of a belover,
hands empty but eyes brimmed with colour.
Thy are the nucleus of Jannat e Jahan,
Don't they know why Taj was built by Shah e Jahan?
    Shall I call you the fragrant rose,
Which pulmonates every bulb in the royal lawn?
Or Shall I call you the moum candle?
Which crumble but enlightens eye apple.
Shall I call you the Diwan of great poets,
who scribble thousand pages and earned fame?
Or Shall I call you the Al-Nisa,
Sent by the Heavens,
for the lady of earth and the mother of Isa?
    My dear women,
Thy are the spine of mankind,
Whose womb forbears the weight of generations.
Thy are the dolphin: who never sleep,

Agile and playful, though in waters deep.
O Madame!
Qays fought for the wasal of Laila,
Didn't they see, his fragmented world?
Shakespeare's Romeo had been an ordinary man,
If Juliet had not met his eyes at a night ball.
Thou are the Hamsar, for tender heart of Farhad, Whose
Longing eyes walked over several miles,
to built the bridge, only to connect with Shireen.
Didn't they see why Farhad died,
Just to unite in horizons with Nazanin!
Do they deny, the existence of Laleshwari,
didn't her being influenced Sheikh ul Alam?
With her Vaakhs, she resonated in the Karewas,
bitter and tough, sweet and soulful.
Yes, she is Lal Ded or Lalla!
Habba weaved 'Lol' when Yousuf left,
called off her sufferings when she said:
"Waervaen sith vaari chas no, chaari kar moen maalino"
I am unhappy in my husband's home,
Relieve me from suffering, O my father's clan.
Takhleeq-e-Khuda, O woman!
Thy are created of the same mud,
that smells no other from the men.
Thy have the same Lord to which they worship.
Thy have the same Heaven, to which they enter.
Thy have the same place, on which they live.
Thy are Flowery, Fragrant and Fragile.
An entire Universe in a human form!

CHAPTER ELEVEN

Entry no.11

About the Author:

Mamata Bhokare is an educator and has been working in this field for 20 years now. Possessing Masters degree in Botany, she has always been an academician. Mostly surrounded by youngsters, she has acquired the qualities of exploring and being inquisitive all the time. Writing and painting is her passion and she considers herself as a learner in those fields. Expressing through words, she enjoys writing simple prose and poems in Hindi and English. Currently she is working on her Fiction 'Under the blue sky' which is the manifestation of the complex relation between a young couple in love, who are mentally disturbed. Her Hindi poem 'Jung' expresses the strong feelings of a rape survivor and has been awarded and is ready to be published in an anthology across the country soon. She could be reached on Instagram handle @mkbhokare

Empowered Within

Glued to the stove,
Wiping the floor,
Serving the bowls,
What next to go?
Changing the diapers,
Making the bed,
Cleaning the mess,
Oh, this is what I do?
    I am born for more,
Traverse and explore,
My abilities and skills,
Can I just let it go?
Who is stopping me?
The society, the public?
No, no it's me, No No, it's me..
    Some will say you can't,
Some will say you won't,
Who's to decide?
Yes, yes it's me, yes yes it's me...
Ladies first, bull shit !
Has equality got a shift?
Feminism mistaken,
As misandry to be...
    I have the power
To bloom a life within,
Do I need to validate
My existence herein?
I have the might,
I have the courage,
Who will stop me?
To empower within
To empower within.

CHAPTER TWELVE

Entry no.12

About the Author:

Shah Samar Imtiyaz, is a talented researcher, writer, and host from KP road Anantnag, Kashmir. She recently completed her post-graduation at the Sher e Kashmir University of Agriculture Science and Technology.

In addition to her academic pursuits, Samar is a published author and poet. She has written the book "The Rainbow," which explores the various forms of love and its power to bring about positive change. She has also co-authored the books "Mated Talk-Hell or Heaven" and "Life in Fervour." In addition to writing, Samar has hosted various programs and podcasts, and even presented her research at an international conference at Kashmir University.

But Samar's talents and achievements don't stop there. She was shortlisted as a brand ambassador for Lemon ideas (innovation cell), and her innovative idea was selected among the top 150 globally. She has also won numerous awards and certificates for her academic and creative endeavors, including a second-place finish in a district-level competition for Abacus Learning of Higher Arithmetic's,

a ninth-place ranking in the National Aeronautical Space Administration Olympiad, and an honor grade from RSM (Pg) College Bijnour for qualifying in a horticultural quiz.

Currently, Samar is working on her next book, with the goal of reaching and inspiring readers with her uplifting message that there is still hope and goodness in the world. She believes that writing for the betterment of others is more important than causing harm and division. She could be reached on Instagram handle @_shah_samar_

The Prison of Heartache

She was put into the sphere where new perception in the peepers was not just the grime on the pupil.
It was something that put her into the solitude of perplexion.
The dusty vintage was more alluring than the scintillating modern.
The facts seemed acrid whilst the antique seemed outdated.
Changing dresses seemed terrible whilst changing faces cool.
It wasn't where she contemplated being appertained to!

She had a gooey core, with naïve eyes that were famished for love and approbation.
They knew she would stay in the sphere whilst they shatter her fragile heart
She was the sovereign of her Fathers red empire whilst they made her the thrall.
Thrall of accepting what she ne'er wanted to!
The burden of tocher buried her dreams and engraved her heart with nothing but agony, and abhor towards the

humanity!
The one she thought to be the velvet in her ways, turned out to be the rugged carpet.
She sighed, The sunny heart of mine started crying!
I am offtracked from my life,
Why did that loving breeze turn out to be the toxic one and then hurted my puffs?
Why did my heart even break when I thought it was safe in your hands?
It has now shattered completely.

My heartbeats have now lost the rhythm.
I have lost my identity, even my silhouette has deserted me!
I don't recognize myself anymore,
where should i go?
I don't find the pertinent way.
The fate of my heart is not good.
It didn't go as i thought.
What seemed to be an ocean from far, was actually a mirage of sand.
The fate betrayed me,
The palm lines didn't turn out to be impressive as well, The fate betrayed me, the fate betrayed me!

She had none to hold her hand and no shoulder to cry upon!
She was thought to be filthy,
But they forgot that she was never made from the soil.
She was made from the rib of a man
That ran near his wild heart,
Just to protect and be more near to it.
All she had was hope in her womb
That was too told to give-up upon!
Nevertheless, she never lost the hope,
The hope that would alter everything.

Because she knew, she, and her apple of an eye,
Never belonged to where they were put,
the prison of heartache.

CHAPTER THIRTEEN

Entry no.13

About the Author:

Medhat Zaffar resides at Barzulla, in Srinagar. She is persuing BA(LLB) from the college affiliated with kashmir University. Furthermore, she infuses the hue of literature in her write-ups by learning and reading more about it. Moreover she is a proficient speaker which enables her to decode the message or to comprehend the message of another person in a more clearer and lucid form since language is something that connects and helps in smooth functioning of any community. She is fetching the accountability to make everything subtle and held herself responsible for the smooth functioning of the organization.

Women

The sighs in the eyes,
Befalling the dusk of
Autumn that "she" carries.
In the gallows of her heart,

Unraveling, unveiling the
Unceasing ponds of pain.
Slithering from her chest
To croon the treachery of
her fate!
Crumbled by the
Oceans of miseries and grief,
Witness the catastrophe
Of wilderness and taboos
of society crippling 'her'.
Unshackle her from the
Fetters of cruelty and grief.
Fo us ! She is a women
One who bear(s) a men!

CHAPTER FOURTEEN

Entry no.14

About the Author:

Dr Mehjabeen is a passionate and dedicated human being and a global ambassador for Mental health issues. She has educated 500 kids in the rural areas and is running her own school, offering free education for underprivileged kids. She could be reached on Instagram handle @dr_mohammedmehjabeen

She has won several accolades like

1) Mahila Ratna Award.

2) ASIAS INFLUENTAL WOMEN AWARD as an excellence psychologist.

3) WOMEN INTERNATIONAL ICON AWARD (as Diffrence maker)

4) INDIAN WOMEN HISTORY MUSEUM REWARDED CERTIFICATION (as a mental & health ambassador)

5) MADAD FOUNDATON REWARDED CERTIFICATION (for contributing in aid to Covid-19 patients).

6) ASIA EDUCATION AWARDS (Best Psychologist)

7) INDIA'S TOP 50 INFLUENTIAL WOMEN (in Outstanding Contribution in Mental Health Wellness)

8) WOMEN OF SUBSTANCE AWARDS (on international

women's day) as a CHANGE MAKER.

Fairy Tale

When she walks with her noises,
The nature talks to her like 'hey beautiful it's you and you carrying yourself lovably'
With her confidence, she is blessed and crowned with treasures of possibilities.
Her notoriousness says that she can be anything!
Description of her pain is unmeasurable,
Like her silken wavy hair falling on her face and still she give a smile to cheer up others.
She can handle any situation like an artist,
and paint the beautiful colours of life,
with a meaningful picture!
She is unique and so caressing,
when is a mother protects her skin.
She is a sunrise, giving light to other's life.
Her womb is always safe to her loved ones.
Her strength is love!
Thou she is sad,
Thou she is happy
Thou she is in trouble,
Thou she is challenging.
Her smile is unique.
She is always strong and make her life complete,
by facing challenges and struggles.
No one can replace her as she is in many roles:
A mother, wife, daughter, sister and what not!
Proud to be toughest walnut.

Nothing gonna change her focus.
Her future is her goals and her life is everything to her soul.
Dedicated her life to the beautiful colours of bonds.
She is a rainbow, where every colour reflect her different role.
Respect her : god has made her powerful!
Let us celebrate her every moment as she is very precious and important.
Love her ; care her ; acknowledge her.
She is born to be very special "the women; the women"

CHAPTER FIFTEEN

Entry no.15

About the Author:

Zeenat Najar is from district Srinagar and has persued her masters in English Language and Literature from University of Kashmir. She loves reading books particularly novels. She likes creative writing in the form of prose and poetry. However, she focusses mainly on topics that show the beauty and teachings of Islam, importance of human kindness towards fellow beings and importance of education of women (both religious and worldly) for the foundation and prosperity of a beautiful society. She is a teacher by profession and her speciality is teaching English as a second language .

She believes that her schooling has always played a pivotal in her life and the career she choose. She is thankful to all the teachers who have taught her throughout her life, particularly her school teachers and University Professors (department of English). She believes that a teacher's influence remains with a student for a longer part if his /her life, therefore, she wants to be a role model for her students. She always aspires to become as good as her school teachers had been. She aims to become a better muslimah, better human being and a better learner of the treasure of the knowledge given to children of Adam by Allah in the form of vast literature present in the world. She could be reached at najarzinat123@gmail.com and on Instagram @Zeenat.najar.9

She is currently preparing for the competitive exam.

She loves a verse from the poetry of Iqbal, which she believes gives her motivation to do better everyday.

منزل سے آگے بڑھ کر منزل تلاش کر
مل جائے تُجھ کو دریا تو سمندر تلاش کر

"Women Empowerment may be defined in several ways, including accepting women's viewpoints, making an effort to seek them and raising the status of women through education, awareness, literacy, and training....." ~*Wikipedia.*

So, taking the above definition of wikipedia, I presume that it is what we as women mostly believe what "Women Empowerment " is. However, there may be different opinions and beliefs regarding the same. Nevertheless, it does give to some extent a general idea of the same topic and I would like to begin my article with raising a pivotal question about the topic itself.

Why do women need to be empowered? So beginning my discussion with answering the same question, I feel that it is because we live in a patriarchal society where women are oppressed in different ways '' ironically " starting from her birth itself. Women have been suppressed everywhere in the world_ as history tells us, and continues to suffer_if not everywhere, but somewhere for sure_ even in the 21st century.

Despite all the modernization, we need something more to treat women rightly and it can only be done by first understanding this thing at a deeper level.For a authentic or reliable example I would like to take the example of my own kashmiri culture and society.

In kashmir when a girl is born people give sort of condolences to the concerned parents ;instead of congratulating them! With this starts the cycle of events or we could say all the widespread evil in the society in the form of mistreating women. The need of the hour ,therefore ,is to go back to the teachings of Islam,which has empowered women back at a time when the girl child was buried alive!

So, there is ,indeed ,a solution to this evil which is learning our religion and understanding the rights given by Almighty Allah in the Quran and the teachings of the last Prophet and Messenger of Allah,Prophet Mohammad ﷺ . Our creator, Allah has attributed a whole Surah in the Quran to women, viz;(Surah An -Nisa), "Nisa " is an Arabic word which means "woman".

In another chapter of the Quran Allah says:

"We have enjoined on man kindness to his parents; in pain did his mother bear him, and in pain did she give him birth" (Quran 46:15; Surah Al _Ahqaf verse 15)

The Prophet Muhammad ﷺ said : Your Heaven lies under the feet of your mother (Ahmad, Nasai)

Jabir ibn Abdullah reported: The Messenger of Allah, ﷺ said :“Whoever has three daughters and he cares for them, he is merciful to them, and he clothes them, then Paradise is certainly required for him.” It was said, “O Messenger of Allah, what if he has only two?” The prophet ﷺ said,

“Even two.” Some people thought that if they had said to him one, the Prophet ﷺ (PBUH)would have said even one.

Abu Huraira reported that a person came to Allah’s Messenger, Prophet Mohammed ﷺ and said : Who among the people is most deserving of a fine treatment from my hand ? He ﷺ said : Your mother. He again said : Then who (is the next one) ? He ﷺ said: Again it is your mother (who deserves the best treatment from you). He said: Then who (is the next one) ? He ﷺ said : Again, it is your mother. He (again) said: Then who? Thereupon He ﷺsaid: Then it is your father (Sahih Muslim) .

Messenger of Allah Prophet Mohammad ﷺ said:"Whoever is tried with something from daughters, and he is patient with them, they will be a barrier from the Fire for him." (Jami` at-Tirmidhi)

Even ,in the last sermon Prophet ﷺ directed the Ummah to treat women well. Prophet ﷺ said:
"......People, it is true that you have certain rights with regard to your women but they also have rights over you. Remember that you have taken them as your wives only under Allah’s trust and with His permission. If they abide by your right then to them belongs the right to be fed and clothed in kindness. Do treat your women well and be kind to them for they are your partners and committed helpers... (The Last Sermon Of Prophet Muhammad ﷺ _Sahih Muslim and Bukhari) .

Just by citing a few quranic references and few hadith of the Prophet ﷺ,it is quite evident that the women have been empowered by Allah and His Messenger ﷺ starting from her birth till her last breath. However, the need of the hour is that men learn those responsibilities towards women folk and women learn their rights given to them by Islam , so that our homes in particular and society in general becomes a tranquil abode for women to live.

9 798890 024398

Printed by Libri Plureos GmbH in Hamburg,
Germany